S. AGGARWAL'S

THE
PERFECT
BOOK FOR
IMPERFECT
COUPLES

*The Most Powerful Approach To Build a
Happy Relationship For Life*

ACKNOWLEDGEMENT

Firstly I would like to thank the Almighty for making this book possible. I can't thank my parents enough for making me the person I am today, where I feel I have something I can share with the world, with its people to make their lives a little better. I wish to thank my husband who rested his faith in me, that I have the flair for writing, and also motivated me whenever I felt low and was always behind me when I tried to procrastinate. It would not have been possible if it wasn't for you, my love. A big thanks to my son who lent me his support by not disturbing me and also excusing me for the 'less time' that I gave him all the while I was busy working on this book.

Thanks to all the readers who gave me a chance to share my opinions with them and who chose to head on this life-changing journey with me.

My heartfelt thanks to all of you.

CONTENTS

WHO SHOULD READ THIS BOOK

All those people out there who think they probably messed up in finding for themselves a perfect life partner. For all those who think that their ideal partner is hiding behind door number two. For all those who are in dilemma of a relationship that they feel they can neither keep nor discard and most importantly those people who have the slightest hope that maybe one day they can be a perfect couple- this book is for you.

This book does not tell you about how to find a perfect life partner nor does it give you the traits to be one. It does not advise you to do complex studies and research about your partner and then come to action based on the conclusions you draw about your partner's habits, nature, or character. It does not ask you to change yourself in a way that is liked by your partner.

This book does not give you 10 ideas or 5 tips or 7 secrets to make your marriage work. I believe such ideas and tricks don't usually find much application and are soon abandoned and forgotten. I believe one thing that can work is the reconditioning of your mind.

'Our mind is the real master' we act according to what it says. So, if we learn to control it with the right thoughts, it signals us to work accordingly. Napoleon Hill says, "You either control your mind or it controls you". So, here in this book, you get to know a beautiful approach regarding your relationship with which if you regularly condition your mind, it becomes a mindset, and with that right mindset, you can never go wrong with your relationships.

A negative mind can never give you a positive life. However much you try but no secrets or tips are going to work if you are not thinking right about your relationship. So, what matters is your thought process. When you start thinking and saying what you really want, your mind pulls and shifts you in that direction. This is how mind reconditioning works and we can change our mindset to change our relationships and also change our lives, for the better- and that's what this book aims to do.

So, if you are in to proceed with me on this journey where we learn to create beautiful thoughts that in turn create a beautiful mind that helps you create a strong relationship that's meant to last forever, then you are 'Welcome'!

WHY IT'S THE PERFECT BOOK

I call it the perfect book because I feel it is practical, doable, and achievable. Anything that's theoretical and does not have much practical application finds low or no results. The approach used in this book is very simple and can be easily applied to our lives to get great results.

If you feel you are an imperfect couple, it's totally fine. Imperfections are good. Perfect is boring.

But if you feel your relationship is imperfect, here we will try to make it perfect. Perfect with all its ups and downs, its joys and sorrows, its good and bad times; but one that brings a smile to your face when you think about it.

Thank you for picking up this book. It won't let you down.

I hope it truly turns out to be 'The Perfect Book' for you.

YOUR PROMISE TO ME

I'm not here to make a perfect couple out of the imperfect one (as you think you are). I'm here to make you a happy couple. I'm here to tell you how you can make your partnership last an eternity.

Through this book, I'm determined to change your mindset about the most important things in life. I'm determined to make you believe that you can be a happy couple. I'm determined to save relationships from failing and I'm also determined to make you determined about putting in efforts to make your relationship better. But for that, I need a promise.....

"Promise to put in the effort. Promise me that you will do all it takes to make your relationship better. Promise me that you will strive and not give up till the end. Promise me that you will not just read what this book says, but try to stick to it and apply it in your life".

If you promise me that, I also promise you something.............

"I promise to you that you will not repent. I promise that you will find that your efforts have paid off. I promise you a better relationship. I promise you a happier relationship. I promise you a long-lasting relationship".

Close your eyes. Put your hand on your heart and say:

"I Promise to put in the effort"

Affirmations have the power to motivate you to take action, stay positive and just keep going without getting demoralized or deviated from your goal. If you wish to stay motivated all day, get your free set of beautifully designed printable affirmations, suitable for framing. Just drop me a mail at:

shrutifeb08@gmail.com

If you wish to stay accountable in your journey, you can pick up "The Perfect Workbook – because relationships need some effort" by S. Aggarwal (available on amazon) which apart from reminding you the daily affirmations also helps you to make sure you are doing those little acts every single day to nourish your relationship. It is a nine-week workbook with daily practices, weekly goals to keep track of your progress and final relationship report to make sure your efforts pay off. It is easy to use and would require just five minutes of your day. I'm sure that's not too much of time!

Just remember you promised to put in the effort.

THE DEFINITION OF PERFECT AND IMPERFECT

Perfect and imperfect are actually very relative terms and there is no clear-cut definition for the two. What is perfect to one may not be that perfect to another and to still another, be totally imperfect. It is actually a matter of perception.

The same goes with the term 'Perfect couple'. I wanted to see if I could find a definition of this term. Maybe some learned one had managed to figure out what it actually is, so I decided to Google it. Look what I found. Wiki says –"A "perfect couple" is a happy couple who enjoy time together, value each other, and maintain a strong bond". It's as simple as that. And you thought marriage was a really complicated thing.

Although this may sound effortless, still millions of couples find this little thing unattainable and are struggling to thrive in almost every part of the globe. The divorce rates are getting higher and two out of every ten couples are going through relationship stress, toxic relations, arguments, criticism, and conflicts every day in their married lives, and find their lives screwed up. It is then they start to think that maybe they made a wrong decision in life, a wrong choice. Maybe they are not a "PERFECT COUPLE"........

WHAT ACTUALLY IS A PERFECT COUPLE?

"Far too many people are looking for the right person, instead of trying to be the right person"- Gloria Steinem.

While it is always important to pair up with a compatible person: compatibility doesn't just mean sharing the same interests or opinions.

Here, I would like to quote my personal experience. I am married for twelve years and you could say we are a 'perfect couple'. My husband and I are people from two different planets, really. While my husband is an introvert, I am a really outgoing person and like to socialize a lot. While my husband is very patient and calm, I have a bad temper and am extremely impatient (Although I have worked on it now). I am a foodie and an art lover and it's a no-no for my husband. While he tends to linger over problems and keep thinking about them over and over again, I am a solution seeker. I could go on and on about our differences but I'd like to end it here- 'We love each other'.

Wiki goes on to say, "No couple is truly "perfect," but you and your partner can become your own version of a perfect couple". Happy relationships can be had between two totally different people who are in no way compatible on paper. What matters most is the compatibility in their "Approach" toward their relationship.

THE MOST POWERFUL APPROACH

Let's start by revising the last line of the previous chapter. It said- What matters most is the couple's approach to their relationship. Now many of you would question, what approach? How I should look at my relationship? Or how I should treat my partner? Or what method should I follow in my relationship? What the hell is this approach?

You don't need to remember a long list of dos and don'ts for being in a relationship. God, you're building a relationship, not a rocket to land on Mars. Neither do you want complicated algorithms for every situation in your marriage.

The internet is filled with a hundred different things you can do to be a perfect couple. There are thousands of books on relationships. You can get great ideas from relationship experts or counselors. Not to forget the free advice from relatives and friends.

These are but a fine bouquet of florid, sweet words or phrases like a strong bond, mutual trust, respect, love, and so on, which we all already know. There's nothing new about it. The problem is- What to do about them? How do you achieve them? However much we try, these are abstract nouns that don't seem to exist in this real world. If that's how you feel, I have something for you.

That's what I call 'the most powerful approach'.

'Five ways to become a happy couple' or 'seven signs of a perfect couple' are good reads but these things cannot be applied when it comes to actual life. You won't remember them in the first place and even if you do, you won't know which advice would work in which situation. When a couple is into an argument or a conflict, there is very little or you can say probably no chance that they remember what they read in those 'five things to do...and so on. Here it's their mindset that plays the actual role. So what we have to concentrate on is changing that mindset.

What you need is a simple concept that you keep in your mind always and it's always going to help you, whatever the situation may be. And that is- *"RELATIONSHIP COMES FIRST"*.

RELATIONSHIP COMES FIRST

Our every THOUGHT is followed by a FEELING. So if you're not feeling nice, you have to stop and check- what have you been thinking? Your feelings over a period of time, created on the basis of your thoughts, develop your ATTITUDE- about people, situations, work, or the world. Your attitude decides your ACTION. Any action done repeatedly becomes a HABIT. All your habits put together make your PERSONALITY.

So everything eventually started from your thoughts. It is this thought process that we need to work on. We always think we need to do things outside to change the way we feel inside. The reality is we need to change how we feel inside to change things outside. According to Dr. Wayne Dyer, "Your thoughts are seeds that you plant".

This is one thumb rule you always need to remember in marriage. You may be in any situation in your life like a heated argument, some major disagreement or a situation demanding sacrifice, or even a cold war. You can end the crisis and put your relationship back to life if you only remember that-Relationship comes first.

Once you bring this little thought to your mind, things will automatically start flowing in the right direction. You will know what to do, what's right to do.

It's like pressing the system reboot button. Believe me, this has worked for me and can work for everyone else too.

The most powerful approach:

. You need to change your thought process to be able to bring positive changes to your life.

. Nourish your brain with the thought – 'Relationship comes first'

. It is like pressing the system reboot

HOW DOES IT WORK?

Every couple goes through difficult times. Times of disagreements, fighting, criticizing, quarreling. Whenever we are in such a situation, both partners are thinking negatively. Their minds are filled with unconstructive thoughts which if allowed to flow can be extremely damaging to their relationship. Most of us in such a situation keep lingering to these thoughts, which magnify the negativity. The exchange of words from the other end adds fuel to the fire which in turn becomes destructive to the relationship. This can eventually paralyze the relationship.

Often when we sit back and think over those situations with a calm, relaxed mind; we realize that they arose out of very small issues. Often couples start with a very small problem, but it grows and grows because we do not cut away the negative thoughts.

Now imagine a button that when pressed would stop this flow of negativity. The fight would end and save your relationship from breaking. You have that button now. It's just this thought that you create in your mind that, "My relationship comes first". If you love your partner, if you want to spend your life with him and you are truly inclined towards keeping your relationship going, then you have to understand that your opinions, your ego, your profession, or whatever that's causing trouble in your relationship is important; it's not as important as to come in the way of your relationship or damage it. Remember everything else can wait. You have to prioritize your relationship above everything else. Yes, believe me, you won't regret it.

I have done this a hundred times and always saved my day from getting ruined, and probably my relationship too. And I am glad I did that. So all you need to do is press that button but you now need to understand when to press it.

RELATIONSHIP COMES ABOVE WHAT?

Now let me explain this to you. Suppose you have lots of housework to be done within a limited time. What do you do? You prioritize your tasks based on how important they are or which one needs to be done first and which can wait. Similarly in life, you need to decide your priorities, and here is where your relationship should always come first.

Every role that you play in life is important, but not as important as your relationship. Because relationships are the basis of your life. If your relationships are peaceful and filled with love, everything else will be sorted. You will be happy and more accepting and filled with positivity to play all other roles of your life well.

On the other hand, if your relationship is unhealthy, your entire life will be in turmoil. This is because we are human; we are driven by feelings, by emotions. If our heart aches our mind won't function properly. So, it's extremely important to keep your relationship in the first place.

Another reason why I say relationships should come first is because relationships are like a glass ball. They are vulnerable. They need your utmost care, lest they get broken.

Now let us consider all those things that we generally tend to put above our relationships and thus our relationships suffer.

#1 PROFESSION

Marc and Jessie went to high school together. They always liked each other. Both of them were like-minded, ambitious, and career-oriented. They kept seeing each other even as they completed their higher studies. As the two had so much in common, there was no reason they could not have a very happy married life. They tied a knot.

A few months passed. Both were extremely happy. They had made the best decision of their lives. It seemed that their union had turned all the fortune towards them. Marc was working in a corporate firm as a graphic designer. His company paid him well and he was able to climb his career ladder pretty quickly.

Jessie was the team leader at a market research company and soon became the vice-president of her company.

Life was looking great. Financial abundance often sets all other problems apart. They were quite happy. They bought a new house which was much bigger than the one in which they lived before and everything seemed perfect.

But with time everything that seemed so perfect on the outside, started getting 'not so perfect' inside. Something was strangely missing. What was it? They had now almost everything money could buy. But what they could not buy was, "Quality time".

Both came home with an extraordinary level of stress from a highly demanding work schedule. They found it challenging to make time for each other.

Especially Jessie whose job required ten to twelve hours of a day and also traveling a couple of days a week. Sometimes they didn't talk for days. Their lifestyle and work schedule were killing their marriage.

Marc soon started to realize the emptiness in their relationship and tried to talk to Jessie. But Jessie was too absorbed to be able to understand the problem and only said that Marc was over-reacting.

Marc started getting frustrated. He was not getting any attention from his wife. Every day he got back home not to find Jessie at home. He took to drinking alcohol to erode loneliness and desperation. He started misbehaving with Jessie, shouting and yelling at her.

Jessie on the other hand comprehended that Marc was jealous of her career growth. The rift began to deepen and they were now arguing and fighting all the time. Their marriage was in troubled waters.

Many couples are facing similar issues these days. Problem- Profession is being placed above relationship. When your professional life becomes so demanding that you fail to give quality time to your partner, your partner is bound to feel neglected and left out. A marriage can never be great if the partners do not spend enough time with each other and healthily interact with each other. Giving prime importance to our profession can leave our relationships deprived of quality time.

Of course, our careers are important and relationships also thrive well when backed by sound financial support. But putting your relationship at stake only to climb the success ladder is not the right thing to do.

Such people when questioned regarding not spending time with their family often defend themselves by saying that they work day and night for their family. Yes, that's true. They are doing it for their family, for meeting their needs, for their comforts or better status, and their 'happiness'. But in that process 'happiness' is getting lost. They are creating more scars in this process than they think they can heal with the wealth they accumulated.

For all those career enthusiasts who want to see themselves at the top of the ladder; please answer one question-

"Do you want to see yourself at your dream position alone, or do you want your partner, your family to be with you when you are there?"

And there, you have answered yourself. Now you have to decide what comes first-profession or relationship?

Often people think, 'When I'll become successful or I reach a particular position, I'll have enough time for my family'. My dear friend just let me know when that day dawns. Time will never come. You have to make time and you will do that only when you prioritize your family above everything else. Even out of our busiest schedules, we always manage to find time for all those things that we actually value. 'I don't get time' is actually your way of saying 'Forget it, it's not that important'.

Moreover, as I said earlier, it's all about our mindset. If we have placed our career above relationships in our mind, nothing will change even if we reach the desired position in our career as that craving for going higher and higher will never end. And we will never have enough to be satisfied.

WHAT IS TO BE DONE?

The two best methods of solving the problems arising in your marriage due to your career or profession are - Communication and Quality time.

1. COMMUNICATION

Different work schedules, managing home and work, career stress, or feeling exhausted when back home; whatever the reason be, there is no compensation for communication. A long-lasting relationship is built on effective communication and a collaborative effort from both partners.

IMPORTANCE OF COMMUNICATION

When we get into a relationship we feel extremely attracted and too much in love. But this 'butterflies in stomach' feeling wouldn't last forever. It fades off with time and so does the vibe that you shared in the early days of your relationship. This is where communication plays a major role. To keep the love between you and your partner strong. Honest communication between you and your partner will not only remind each other of the reason for falling in love but also increase respect and love for each other.

Honest and open communication also helps to build trust. You learn to confide in your partner and feel secure. It also helps to know each other better. You can get a better understanding of your partner's likings, their shortcomings, their interests, their moods. This helps you at every step of life as there is nothing better than knowing your partner well.

You not only get ample opportunities to learn about your partner but can also learn new things in life as each of us is different and have a different set of qualities, interests, and skills which we can learn from each other.

Communication helps in strengthening the bond of love, care, and affection between the couple and is one of the vital ingredients that nourish a relationship.

. Share your experiences daily

A study published in psychological science found that couples feel closer when they have shared experiences. So when you share everyday experiences, you share numerous stories and ultimately build up a bank of shared experiences that help you feel closer together.

Communication on a daily basis is very important else you start building a wall between yourselves. You need to talk to each other, listen to each other's problems, sympathize with them or give them encouragement or advice or sometimes just laugh at the problems which seem out of your control. Communicate like real partners, partners in joy and partners in sorrows. Also, communicate like friends, accept their mistakes, not judge them, and get involved in a light-hearted conversation.

Believe me, such a daily ritual will soon become a habit and you will be craving to get back home to share your experiences (happy, sad, or funny) with your partner.

. Ask questions

Asking your partner questions helps you get to know your partner, establish trust, boundaries, and intimacy as well as learn about your partner's communication style. Our genuine questions show interest and that we value what our partner experiences. It conveys to our partners that we listen and are genuinely interested in what they are talking about. It increases the flow of conversation and makes it double-sided.

Now asking questions can mean two things. Firstly, when your partner is sharing an experience with you, you need to ask questions or at least respond by nodding your head or slightly leaning forward to show that you are interested. This is very important as if a speaker does not feel he's being heard, his interest to talk would decline.

Secondly, asking deeper questions regarding your relationship sometimes can build insight into your relationship, help you to understand the flaws, and also build a stronger relationship. Questions such as - what is the best thing about us? Or what do you think we can improve in our relationship? Or what makes us feel happy together? are questions that can help you improve your relationship and you can mend or repair any damages before they are too big to spoil your relationship completely.

. Show your love daily

This is very important. Saying 'I love you' more often. Very often we skip saying these words as we assume that our partner knows them and we need not repeat them all the time. But believe me, these words can do wonders.

The happiest couples express their love to each other every single day. Finding love and security in your partner gives you a feeling of fulfillment and makes you feel safe and loved.

 Showing love doesn't only mean saying 'I love you' all the time. Greet your partner every day with a hug or a kiss. Ask them about their day. Hold your partner's hand and tell them how wonderful they are or how happy you feel to be with them. Give your partner a little compliment. You can also try putting a small note expressing your love.

I have seen an elderly couple doing so. The lady put a note in her husband's car or sometimes his office bag. You can just imagine the strength of the message conveyed by doing such a thing. It's more than merely saying it. It's bound to bring a smile to the recipient's face. And that feeling of being loved will linger for a much longer time.

. Make physical contact

Physical contact such as touching your partner, stroking their arm, or holding hands while talking makes communication better as it makes the speaker feel loved and secure and enables him to speak what he feels. The science behind this is that such low-intensity stimulation of the skin promotes and releases a hormone called oxytocin. This is the love hormone that promotes bonding and empathy in romantic partners. It also acts as an anti-stress agent and promotes cooperative behavior.

On the other hand, there are certain times or matters in which communicating becomes very difficult. The partner feels hesitant to talk. In such a situation, physical touch can boost the speaker's confidence and give him the sense of security that he can confide in him.

Communicating well with each other is the best recipe for a happy marriage. All you need to do is be open and honest with your partner. Being honest means telling your partner when you feel some issues need to be talked about. It also means admitting when you were wrong and apologizing instead of making excuses. Honesty not only helps to foster genuine open communication between you and your spouse but also helps to build trust.

So we should try to make communication an important ritual in our daily schedule. Prioritizing your partner above work and daily chores and giving them your full and undivided attention will make your relationship last an eternity. Remember – relationship comes first.

. Remember to express you love every single day.

. Your partner is perhaps your best friend. Share what you feel, with them.

2. QUALITY TIME

There is no doubt about this one. Spending quality time together is one of the major factors that can make your relationship last long.

But for most of us, time together and particularly quality time can be quite difficult to find. Partners are often found struggling between work and home schedules, grocery shopping, and childcare. If they get any little time from these, they are still discussing or planning about the same.

But it's not unachievable. If we are truly inclined to make our relationship healthy and we truly love and value our partner, we can do it.

Quality time does not always mean going on romantic dates or holidays. And it need not scoop you out of your work or other schedules. It need not be very lengthy or complicated. It can be as simple as sharing a cup of coffee every morning. It actually means spending time with your partner without interruptions or any distractions, in which you can emotionally connect with each other.

Your partner is there with you every day and you meet him every morning and evening. But that's not enough. You deserve more from your relationship.

Spending quality time together is a great way to build a friendship. It gives us shared interests and experiences. We get an opportunity to have fun and laugh together and get closer to each other.

Setting time aside regularly for your loved one is a small step that can make a huge impact on your relationship. We all manage and set out time for things that matter to us most, and our relationship is no different.

The benefits of spending quality time together are endless. It can transform good marriages into great ones.

HOW TO SPEND QUALITY TIME WITH YOUR PARTNER

. Try new things together

Doing new things together can be a fun way to connect and keep things interesting. If you've ever wanted to learn to play a new instrument or learn a new language or some form of dance; why not involve your partner in them?

Trying new things together not only helps you learn faster and better because you learn from each other's mistakes; it also builds a healthy relationship by encouraging you to rely on each other for physical and emotional support. Shared hobbies also promote friendship in marriage.

Doing new things together from time to time can be that element of spark in that dying fire of passion in a relationship. You can try doing something that you both enjoy, like watching a new web series together, exploring a new hobby, going to a new restaurant, or simply playing a board game. These new experiences will keep you interested and motivated. These will intensify the emotions in your marriage and help keep you closer.

. Hit the gym together

In case you are finding it difficult to find time, you can involve your partner in activities that you both do, but at different times or different places. In that case, you only need to adjust your timings to match each other. And what better than hitting the gym together?

Most of us go to a gym or a fitness class; so why not do it together? Not only does it helps you to spend time together, but it also encourages and motivates you to do better.

. Cook meals together

Cooking meals often take a lot of time off our schedule. But if you do it together you can enjoy the process. You can have a lot of healthy conversations. You can cook more innovative meals together. You can also compete as to who is a better cook or who completes a task faster, just for the sake of fun.

Cooking together is actually a great idea as on one hand, you share the work and that makes the burden light for one. On the other hand, you get immense time to talk, laugh, and have fun together.

Remember, the dishes are yet to be done. You can do them together too!

. Have regular date nights

Date nights clearly mean couple-time. So it's obvious that it is important for a happy relationship. Regular date nights make way for better and healthy communication. It helps to build intimacy and attachment for each other and decreases stress.

Apart from these, there are a few other reasons why having regular date nights is important. Firstly, when you intentionally set out time for your relationship, you are letting your partner know that they are important to you. Secondly, it allows the couple to enjoy some time together forgetting all worries of their daily lives.

A date night can be simple like a beach walk or just staying at home to cook and enjoy a great meal (just the two of you). At times it can also be elaborate like a classic movie-dinner date when the two of you can dress up and enjoy a great romantic evening.

. Laugh together

Laughing together is a great exercise for a healthy marriage. It is said that laughing for 30 seconds can keep you happy for 3 hours.

Laughing, giggling, and guffawing with your partner increases happiness. Not just in your own life, but in the life you share. Laughter costs nothing, and yet its benefits are massive. Injecting a little humor into your relationship will help it to thrive and survive.

You can watch a funny video together or even crack a joke or even tickle your partner to make him laugh. I know that sounds childish. But, why not? Be a kid.

Couples who laugh together have a stronger bond and are able to overcome stresses and conflicts in their relationship. A sense of humor goes a long way in a relationship. Couples who laugh together, last together.

Romance is one of the most crucial elements of happiness in a relationship. It's that element that makes your relationship different and special from all others.

In the early days of your relationship, just a glance or a mere touch would set the romantic element ablaze. But in the later years when you tend to become more casual and comfortable with each other, romance does not creep up automatically. You have to make efforts to rekindle that fire and to keep it burning.

Often after a few years of marriage, romance seems to fade away as couples get overwhelmed by managing their jobs, kids, household chores, finances, and family. But with some effort, you can bring back the romance in your relationship.

But what does romance mean? A candlelit dinner, music and flowers, moonlit walks, late-night talks...they all spell romance, isn't it? Yes, these are romantic gestures, but romance is also much more than this. Romance is more like an ever-going journey of learning about your partner better. It's a daily choice of being selfless. Doing things for your partner and not expecting anything in return. This is real romance, where you show your partner that you care for them, and also care for everything they care about.

It can be anything that your partner likes. It can be listening to them about their problems without interrupting them or trying to give advice. Showing interest in things they are interested in or doing a few chores to make their burden light without letting them know.

Flowers, music, and dinner can of course be an additional dose of injecting romance into your relationships.

. Do get away whenever you can

Change is important in life to break the monotony and bring a new perspective to life. Let me explain:

Running on a treadmill every day is good, but once in a while going out early in the morning for a walk or a run is even more satisfying. You get a change in the weather, the things you look around. You get to appreciate nature and also come back with a lasting after effect of that relaxing morning session. And that effect probably helps you to be energetic and positive the whole day. That's the importance of change.

Whenever possible, just steal time from your routines and go out. You can go for a movie, a concert or just a long walk. This little change in your routine will add that little spark to light your dull, boring life.

. Continue to flirt

Never stop flirting with your partner! Flirting keeps things interesting and reminds your partner that you find them attractive and intriguing.

Flirting can be as simple as sending a flirty text to your partner unexpectedly in the middle of the day. Your partner surely would not be able to stop themselves from smiling.

The magic of flirting with your partner is such that can be an ultimate mood changer. Suppose your partner gets annoyed over something and complains to you in anger, and you instead of counteracting or defending yourself, give your partner a flirtatious glance and react by saying, "did I tell you that you look really sexy when in anger?" The entire situation can change.

CONCLUSION

Spending quality time with your partner is the ultimate remedy to your relationship problems. The above methods of spending time with each other are sure to create much-needed happy moments in your life.

The small incidents that you collect on each such new venture will become your sweet memories of tomorrow. The memories of these moments spent together will linger throughout your life and bring a smile to your face whenever you recall them.

"Remember, when we joined the Zumba class and you fell, I couldn't stop myself from laughing." "That baking disaster of yours, even the neighbors came over to see what was burning". These are the little pictures of your happy married life that you will always remember and laugh at as you turn over your album of life.

. Giving time to your partner and your relationship should always find place in your to-do list.

. Schedule your we-time for each day and stick to it.

. During this time get involved in meaningful conversation that would help your relationship evolve rather than discussing work or chores.

Let's get back to Marc and Jessie.

Jessie was affected badly by daily conflicts and Marc's drinking habits. This started affecting her at work too. She could no longer concentrate on her work and give her best to it.

It was now that she began to think about what was going wrong in their relationship. She realized that she needed to spend some time with Marc. She decided to take a day off from work every week so that the two of them could spend time together.

Marc at first, did not respond well to Jessie's attempts. Jessie was well aware of Marc's mental condition now and she took very cautious and measured steps to slowly heal the wounds their relationship had suffered. She tried to come home early from work. Although Marc did not show it, somewhere in his heart, he felt happy to see Jessie when he came back from work. Jessie tried to cook things that Marc liked and insist on having dinner together. Marc turned down her offer a few times but a few weeks later became ready for it. Marc was realizing that Jessie was trying to make things right and the best part was that he welcomed her efforts(although hesitantly), instead of clinging to his pain and anger.

Even Jessie was now liking the new life in which they both were heading together. She had realized that her work was important but not more important than her relationship. With continuous efforts and love(and not to forget Marc's support), they brought their de-railed marriage back on track.

What Marc and Jessie realized later in life, should be kept in mind before the damage has been done. This is because unlike Marc and Jessie most couples are unable to come out of such problems easily, they get trapped, frustrated, and finally give up. Always remember that relationships should come above profession.

For now let us go to the next thing that we generally rate above our relationships, and the result of which is that our relationship suffers. That is our egos and conflicts.

#2 EGOS AND CONFLICTS

Josh and Stacey dated for two years before they got married. They had met through a common friend and instantly fallen for each other. Stacey was 21 then and was doing her bachelor's. Josh had already finished college and was looking for a part-time job while he had enrolled in a master's in computer science.

They started meeting on weekends until they were so much in love that they needed to see each other every single day. Josh soon found a part-time job but still, he continued to find time for Stacey. They had spent a considerable amount of time together. So they understood each other well enough to guarantee their marriage would work.

Finally, a few months after josh landed the job of a web developer in a big IT company, they decided to tie a knot.

A simple ceremony with intimate family and just a few friends was followed by a weeklong honeymoon. Everything was just so perfect. They couldn't have imagined anything better.

The first few years of their marriage looked like they were made for each other. They always seemed to agree with each other. Stacey became pregnant and they soon welcomed a baby boy in their new home. Stacey now was a full-time homemaker with a child to look after. She got too engrossed in her jobs as a wife, a mom, and a homemaker. But she found it difficult to strike a balance. Often she felt overburdened and frustrated. She had no time or a life of her own. Her career dreams were the last thing she thought about.

They started quarreling over a lot of things. They regularly hurt each other's feelings, and Josh found himself sleeping on the couch many nights.

They disagreed about finances, delegating chores around the house, childcare, and on and on. They argued about big things and little things. They just couldn't stop arguing. The situation had worsened to the limit that they could not ask each other a question without the other person jumping to conclusions about why that question was asked. It was soon that both started to realize that their relationship needed attention.

Problem- conflicts between partners.
Some of you might be thinking that here the conflict is not the problem, but an outcome of problems between them. But what I would like to bring to your notice is that between

most couples these days, there is no one or two reasons to quarrel. The problem is that they quarrel and quarrel over the weirdest topics right from which direction to squeeze the toothpaste tube to leaving the soaked sponge in the sink to which way to place the toilet roll.

So here we will take conflict as the main problem and the most common reasons why it happens will be dealt with individually. But first, let's delve back into josh and Stacey's case.

Josh was a great provider. He worked hard to get all comforts for his family. His job soaked up his brain like a sponge and he came home every day tired and just retired on the couch watching television to relax his mind. Josh was an organized person himself and complained about Stacey being so disorganized. He comes home every day to find newspapers on the couch, toys on the floor, dirty dishes in the sink, and his wife wearing an apron, feeding their son. Josh didn't like Stacey being so messy and she looks the least attractive to draw his attention away from the newspapers, toys, and dishes. He keeps nagging and criticizing her for it and what follows next is quite predictable.

Stacey also has a hard day at home doing the cooking, laundry and looking after their two-year-old. She, on one hand, feels that she is not getting any kind of help or appreciation for what she does, on the other hand, she finds no time to look after herself or concentrate on her career plans. She blames Josh for not giving time or attention to the family. Whenever an argument starts Stacey defends herself by yelling and crying and saying that their marriage was the biggest mistake of her life. She feels trapped like a laborer with criticism as her wage. She loved her husband but was tired of being hurt by him and was tired of hurting him.

It's not that they didn't love each other. Despite these challenges, they wanted their marriage to last. But none of them knew what to do.

Constant nagging and criticism can ruin any relationship. You don't like your partner's habits and want them to change. Here is the main problem. Why do you always want to change others? As I said earlier, if you really want to change things outside you need to change things inside.

It's your mindset that needs a change. Before starting any argument, just wait for a second and think – do these things matter to me more than my relationship? The mess, the clutter; are they reasons enough to spoil your relationship?

In josh and Stacey's case, both were burdened by their own work schedules and when their partner didn't act the way they expected them to, they nagged and criticized them. But did this actually work? Were they able to change their partner's habits or behaviors in any way? No!

Often couples fight over problems that are not actually problems. Little things can turn on an argument and most of the time couples fight over the same topics over and over again without ever coming to a resolution. It feels like they can't stop fighting and don't know why is it so hard to get along. In such times partners often feel tempted to cut off and move on. But that's called giving up! And we're not here to give up.

You love your partner; it's only the conflicts that are causing problems. "There is no challenge strong enough to destroy your marriage as long as you are both willing to stop fighting against each other, and start fighting for each other."- Dave Willis.

So let's do it. But before that, let's see the most common reasons for conflicts between couples and also how to go about them.

. NOT LIKING PARTNER'S HABITS

Toothpaste cap left open, socks under the bed, empty milk carton in the fridge, toilet seat that's up. All these irritate you and you have a valid reason to feel so. These little things light up big arguments in most households. These little mistakes if become a habit can be actually annoying and need to be talked about. A small change in habits can bring a big difference to the two of you.

Apart from these small habits couples also fight over things they feel are not being done the correct way or at least they feel that the way they do it is correct and the best. Loading technique of dishwasher, folding or placing laundry in the closet, which way to park the car. Oh! Come on. Maybe you are a perfectionist and your partner is not or maybe that's what you feel. These are little things that don't require your attention or perfection. So keep your perfection for other things that are more important and meaningful- like your relationship. The towels will be folded, whether this way or that, but what's more important is to keep peace in your relationship. These daily annoyances will only lead to tit-for-tat squabbles that will spoil your relationship.

Then there are couples like Josh and Stacey, where one of the main reasons for conflict is - not liking partner's habits like Josh not liking Stacey being messy or disorganized. Now being disorganized doesn't actually mean that it's Stacey's habit or liking. I mean who would love to live in a messy or cluttered house? What I mean to talk about are certain things or habits that aggravate you but are not intended to torture you. Maybe they are unintentional and can't be helped. Here I would like to bring an example of Sam and Julie.

Sam and Julie was a couple in CA. They often went out for date nights and social gatherings. But however hard Sam tried to make it, he was always late. Sam was a good and caring partner and he was the one to generally plan date nights but he also had a sucking job and also had to drive an hour back home. This habit of Sam always made Julie go crazy and they ended up arguing. Now, if you were to decide who is at fault, what would you say?

This is what I need to explain. Some tendencies can't be helped although they may seem very annoying to the other person and they are not wrong on their part. Similar to these are habits like your partner's snoring or leaving the toilet smelly. They may be very irritating, but....

How to deal with it?

1. Respect and like each other

Is it possible to love someone without liking him? You may not like the person's habits or behavior or his whole character but still can't help loving him. But such love is short-lived. With time your disliking may overpower your love and it may soon become un-love.

In order to have a relationship that lasts, it's important to like and genuinely respect your partner for the person they are, their achievements, and their qualities.

Wondering what if there is nothing to like about your partner? The problem lies in your perspective. None of us are perfect but each of us definitely has some or the other qualities. You just have to look for those and you will surely find many. So do not forget to notice and encourage what you like in your partner.

Respect is one thing each human wants. Showing respect to your partner will deepen the roots of love and strengthen your bond to last an eternity. Your respect for them may also make them want to try to change for you, the way you wanted them to be.

According to Dr. Gregory Scott Brown, psychiatrist and author of 'The self-healing mind' – "Happiness in a relationship relates to balance, communication, love, and mutual respect. Couples who are happy do disagree from time to time but never lose their core respect for each other".

2. Show appreciation

Learn to replace criticism with appreciation, and see how everything will change magically. Start viewing your partner's qualities instead of focusing on their negative points. Don't look at what has not been done. Look at all that has been done.

Appreciation can do wonders in the worst marriages or disastrous relationships that are on the verge of breaking up.

Maybe you don't take it too seriously. You may think how such a simple thing as a few affirmative words can change the entire scenario. But I'll explain that to you.

In the case of Josh and Stacey which we considered before, both the partners are going through a ruined relationship. There is only nagging, criticism, arguments, blaming each other, frustration, and stress. Imagine if Josh comes home from work and instead of criticizing Stacey for the chores undone, he walks up to her and says, "I am sorry for being so harsh to you. I really appreciate how much effort you put in every day to manage the chores, please tell me how I can help you."

What do you think would be Stacey's reply? Maybe she would get vulnerable and let out her feelings. They can then sit down and discuss their feelings and things can be resolved.

What nagging and criticism did not do, can be achieved by appreciation. You need not say long flattering sentences. Just simple and straightforward compliments like, "you look great", "I love you for cleaning up the garden" or "I really appreciate you for remembering to bring the groceries" can do wonders. Your partner will go all the way to do everything to make you happier and earn your appreciation. Words of affirmation act like the cheerleaders in a race. A student who fails in an examination and is criticized by teachers saying, "You are a loser, cannot achieve anything in life and are good for nothing" is sure to become depressed and would lose any confidence or hope to improve. On the other hand, if he is encouraged by saying, "I know you can do much better than this, you are a good student and just need to work harder. I'm sure you will do better next time" is bound to work hard to keep the trust placed in him. Similarly, you can also bring changes in your partner's habits or behavior with this simple technique of appreciation.

And actually, it is a good habit. People always love to be complimented. Not only in relationships but even at the workplace or at social gatherings; An appreciating person is liked by all. This is more of a personality trait that can be developed to enhance your personal as well as social life.

Verbal compliments or words of appreciation are powerful communicators of love. Such words of affirmation if used regularly can change the emotional climate of your relationship drastically.

Requesting and not demanding

Some of you may think that the only difference between demanding or requesting something is just a change of your tone or maybe adding the word 'please' to it. Although it's true that a humble way of asking something is more accepting. "Could you please do the dishes tonight as I feel exhausted?" is a polite way of asking something but there is something more important than this.

The main difference between a demand and a request is the fact that what reply is being expected from the other side.

Asking for what you want or need becomes a demand if all you expect to hear is a "yes" or you don't want to hear a "No". If a negative reply gets you angry or annoyed it clearly signals to your partner that what you made was a demand and not a request. A request on the other hand is open to both forms of reply from the other person.

So learn to request and not demand from your partner. Sincere requests like, "Can we try to keep the house a little tidy?" or "I would be really happy if you try to be in time" have some chances of being listened to or be worked on but if you choose to demand, then only arguments would follow.

. INADEQUATE ATTENTION OR AFFECTION

This is one major cause of conflicts between couples.

At the beginning of a relationship, we want to be together day and night. It's almost impossible to stay away from each other. But as time progresses, partners begin to take each other for granted. This can lead to arguments if one of the partners feels they are not getting time or attention as their partner likes to spend their free time with friends or maybe scrolling their phones instead of talking or listening to them. Some of them might need more time alone but that drives their partner crazy.

On the other hand lack of affection and intimacy in a relationship starts creating a void wherein partners find it difficult to share their feelings. Their emotional connection weakens. As a result of a lack of affection, the couples are likely to bicker unnecessarily.

Physical intimacy is reduced in the way that there are lesser touches or hugs. They become lonelier and also may try to seek pleasure outside the relationship.

How to deal with it?

1. Increase your communication

As discussed earlier communication is the key to solving all relationship problems. It not only helps you engage with your partner but also makes you understand the changing dynamics in your relationship. Talk about whatever you did or felt during the day, about any incidences that took place at the workplace, something you noticed while driving back home, or any funny moment you came across. Just talk it out. Your relationship needs it. This will not only make you spend time with your partner but also give you the opportunity to share all your joys and sorrows with them.

On the other hand, listening to your partner is equally important. Listen to them while keeping all distractions away and be genuinely interested in what they are talking about.

2. Surprises can work wonders

A little surprise can enliven your dull relationship. After all who doesn't like surprises? If your relationship is going through conflict and the reason is a lack of attention or affection, then this can be the best way to show your love and attention. Just bringing some flowers without a reason and handing them over with a flirty compliment; would be just enough to make your partner blush.

You can also call from work asking your partner not to bother to prepare the meal and that you would order something and enjoy a movie together tonight. It will not only relieve their burden of work but will also help to break the monotony.

And gifts are but the best surprises. I mean everyone loves gifts. But make sure you know their choices else you end up getting into another conflict!

3. Go out

Going out on dates, holidays, day trips, or even shopping together. What your partner seeks from you are your love and your attention, and when we go out we can give our full attention to each other as our minds are relaxed and there are no distractions like household chores, office work, etc. Going out with your partner brings romance and excitement to the relationship.

Remember important dates

One major reason for conflict in relationships is not remembering the dates. The day you met, the day you proposed, the day you decided to get married. Remember them all and try to make them special. This will show that you give attention and importance to your partner and your relationship. Not to mention, forgetting your partner's birthday or your marriage anniversary is a crime worth a life sentence!

Finances are one of the main reasons why arguments arise. Just like mismatched sex drives cause trouble, mismatched financial drives can be equal trouble. One of you might be a spendthrift who pays no mind splashing the cash and worrying about the credit card bills later. While the other one is a saver, a disciplined and regimented person who believes in putting away money for a rainy day and spends money very cautiously.

Although there are no set rules about spending habits, we can't really say what's ideal because it's a matter of one's own abilities, desires, and priorities. Conflicts arise when there are differences in these habits. If both partners have avid spending nature, then there may not be a problem in their relationship although they may have problems paying the bills later. Similarly, if both are hoarders they may be fine but end up not enjoying their life and leaving a fortune to their kids.

For people with two different heads, planning finances and the future can be stressful. And it can get even more stressful if resources are limited, and priorities are varied. Most couples don't spend much time planning their finances or their future and thus they get into trouble. Their priorities and their visions of the future are unclear and unmatched. Because there is no plan in place, things get out of control and conflicts arise.

Not only this, a major reason for conflict is the splitting of bills. Both partners are earning and decide to allocate in some fair or equitable manner their share of expenses and bills. It sounds reasonable but is the cause of major issues such as resentment over individual purchases, dominance, financial infidelity, trust issues, and so on.

Then there are conflicts when there are differences in financial power. Like one partner earns way more than the other, is bound to dominate. Or else one of the partners comes from a wealthy family and the other doesn't. In all such situations, conflicts arise due to power dynamics.

Often financial conflicts arise when couples have or plan to have children. This is because, on one hand, their income decreases due to taking a break from work or reducing hours of work for raising children, on the other hand, their expenses increase considerably because of the new member.

Sometimes the partners also have to look after the needs or expectations of their extended families. For instance, if one of the partner's family faces a severe crisis like an illness or sudden death or things like that, and the partner feels that it's his moral duty to help them. In such cases, conflicts may arise.

Financial problems in relationships have now come out as one of the major reasons for divorce around the world. According to a study conducted by the University of Denver, financial problems contributed to about 36.1% of all the reasons for failed marriages.

How to deal with it?

1. Check your ego

The power play issue can get ugly quickly. Few things bring resentment faster than being made to feel inferior. The partner with more money should always keep in mind the fact that they are a couple, and what's his is ultimately theirs. Their selfish, impulsive, and dominating behavior can ruin their relationship.

2. Focus on your partnership and understand your partner's spending habits

Battling your partner or always trying to change their habits will do you no good. Remember that marriage is a union where both individuals have their own set of opinions, priorities, and habits. Once you focus more on your partnership, you will be able to strengthen your marriage regardless of the financial conflicts you face in your marriage.

A person's attitude towards money primarily comes from their past financial situation. For instance, a person with a poor financial background is bound to be cautious with spending money while a person from a rich background can be easy with money. So instead of always criticizing your partner for their spending habits, try to put yourself in their shoes and understand their habits. By doing so you will be more willing and capable to work a way out together to solve your financial problems instead of always getting into an argument and landing nowhere.

3. Plan your finances together and save for your bigger goals

Work together to decide upon your budget and come up with a plan that both of you can agree upon. Once the plan is made, stick to it with willingness and there should be no resentment on either side.

Apart from your monthly expenses, allocate resources for your bigger goals in life, like a new house or saving for your retirement or children, etc. Work like a team, envision your dreams together and pool in to see your nest being built up slowly and slowly, straw by straw.

4. Be honest and clear

The best way to be sure you and your spouse are on the same page with your joint finances is to talk about them regularly, honestly, and without judgment. Hiding financial information from your partner will neither give you peace of mind nor peace in your relationship.

Remember it's your relationships that ultimately bring happiness and fulfillment to your life, not money. So the next time you differ in your opinions about finance, and want to fight, just close your eyes and think- "What comes first? Relationship or money" Then you can both sit down calmly to discuss things in a positive manner.

The one thing you always need to keep in mind is that you don't need to make money and finances a topic of contention in your life. Instead, you must both support each other and work towards a joint vision for a future together.

. JEALOUSY

This is yet another reason for conflicts between partners.

Jealousy is a natural part of any human relationship. It's easy to get jealous of seeing your partner with a group of friends they could be attracted to or seeing your partner talking to their ex-boyfriend or girlfriend.

But extreme jealousy starts when your partner starts following you everywhere, spies on you, questions your whereabouts all the time, keeps track of where you are or who you are with, or checks your texts or calls. Such jealousy often arises out of the person's own insecurities or low self-confidence or lack of trust in your partner. Extreme jealousy can be a major cause of conflicts between couples as the jealous partner often creates an imaginary space and refuses to listen when told that there is nothing to worry about.

Another form of jealousy is seen when one partner feels that the other partner has more free time for themselves or more friends than they have or a hobby that he really enjoys.

Apart from this career intolerance or being jealous of your partner's career growth is also commonly seen between couples. If one partner has considerable career growth while the other does not, a rift starts to develop between them. Sometimes it's on the part of the one whose career is shooting high when he/she starts to show off their power or position and becomes arrogant or demanding. But mostly the problem arises on the part of the partner whose career has not grown when he starts getting jealous or insecure and his behavior starts getting abnormal and aggressive. This is a sign of danger to the relationship.

How to deal with it?

1. Work on your low self-esteem

Jealousy is but the product of your low self-esteem. Because you lack self-confidence or don't find yourself deserving of your partner, these insecurities start reflecting in the form of jealousy. So to fix this, you need to fix your self-esteem. Stop undermining yourself. Stop comparing yourselves to others. Instead, give yourself some personal time to discover your qualities and your true character.

2. Rebuild your trust

Acknowledging your feelings is the best way to deal with them. Instead of hiding your feelings, you should let your partner know that you don't feel good or comfortable about something. Your partner will have greater respect for you when you disclose your innermost feelings to them and also give them the opportunity to support you or help you out of the situation. Believe in each other and hence rebuild your trust.

3. Learn from your partner

Instead of being jealous of your partner's success, you should try to learn from them. Openly discuss with them their achievement. "Oh! Honey, I'm so happy for you. How did you do this? You've made me proud." This will not only enlighten you with some tips to grow in your own career but will also make your bond stronger by showing them that you really appreciate their achievement. Remember you are partners, and his success is your success and that calls for a celebration not a conflict.

. MISTRUST

Conflicts between couples are also due to trust issues between them.

Mistrust does not only mean doubting the faithfulness of your partner. Often partners undermine each other's abilities and decisions and keep giving them advice constantly. This only gives them signals of mistrust and is never useful and causes conflicts.

How to deal with it?

Believe in your partner's dreams. Trust their decision-making or action-taking abilities in difficult times. Trust that they will do the best in their power for the safety, security, or smooth running of your home and life.

Moreover every person has his own way of doing things. That, it's not your way does not mean that they are doing it wrong. Nor will any person like being treated like a kid by always telling them how, when and what to do.

Sometimes a partner may not have very good decision-making or action-taking abilities. Even in such a case, criticism is of no use. Learn to compliment and complete your partner. You are there to fill each other's voids without even letting them know. Standing strong in areas where you feel your partner is weak. This is what is called a perfect partnership.

It's very common in relationships to have conflicts around sex. The worst thing about sex-related issues is that it strangely becomes all-consuming and spread across all other areas of a relationship.

The most common reason for conflict related to sex is differences in sexual desires. One partner has higher sex drives than the other or one partner wants to have sex more frequently than the other. This can create a lot of conflict in the relationship. If the partner with a higher sex drive tries to initiate sex and is rejected by the other partner, there may be problems. And if this happens often or say two out of three times, then it may lead to frustration or even aggression.

Then there are cases where one partner does not feel any or very low sexual desires. This can often be seen with women after childbirth as they become extra-busy and fatigued, or because they become focused more on their children than marriage. Body changes after childbirth also take a toll and work stress can negatively affect their libido. By the end of the day, sleep becomes their priority over sex.

Distractions are also a major reason for problems in sexual relationships. Children, guests at home, parents living with you, or the burden of chores can be distractions enough to spoil your sex life and also your relationship.

How to deal with it?

Schedule sex

Make your sexual relationship a priority. A busy schedule, workload, or tiredness can always not be an excuse for it. Spouses should re-examine their work schedules and make time available for their partners sexually. You have to try out your own way of bringing sex time into your schedule. If you feel tired and sleepy at night, you can schedule it for the first thing in the morning.

1. Communicate about sex

Communicating about sex is essential for smooth and enjoyable sex life. Be honest in sharing your needs and desires. Tell them what makes you feel good and try to meet midway on your needs so that both partners can feel comfortable about it. Such conversations are vital to avoid building resentment and feelings of rejection.

2. Understand your partner

In most marriages, your spouse is the only person you can have sex with; so as partners it is your moral responsibility to try to understand each other's desires. How and when they like it. Trying your best to satiate each other's desires is important. Surprise them by trying something new and exciting. This can bring back the spark in your dull relationship.

3. Keep the fire of passion burning

Keeping your look physically attractive can keep that fire ignited. Try to be fit and healthy by eating healthy and some exercise. Try new looks or outfits or a changed hairdo or a beard style or a new pair of colored lenses. This way your partner will find something new in you to look at and maybe they want to observe it a little more closely.....

. IN-LAWS

Conflicts with in-laws are almost as inevitable as death. Somehow most of you can never come to similar grounds with them and the reasons may be innumerable.

In some cases, the parents of one or both partners find their son/daughter's spouse unworthy or undeserving. In such cases, they are always trying to find faults in their actions or behavior. They never approve of them and always keep nagging about this to their son/daughter. They may also keep instructing or criticizing their son/daughter-in-law about how to do things.

Another case is when in-laws are too interfering in family matters like how children should be brought up or how to manage finances etc. Such a situation can become very dangerous for the couple as they are bound to get into serious conflicts, after all no one likes interference in personal matters. Here, the partner whose parents are the reason for conflict is in the worst position as on one hand even he finds their interference irritating and on the other hand, he feels hurt when the partner badmouths his parents.

Sometimes the parents are a bit too demanding regarding spending time with them and want to drop in or meet almost every weekend. Maybe they are not wrong in loving their children and wanting to spend more time with them. But it can cause conflicts between the couple as they do not get adequate personal time and space.

Then there is one more and the most profound case, the reason of which is still in the research stage; - mothers-in-law not liking the daughters-in-law and vice-versa and sons-in-law not liking mothers-in-law and vice-versa. Similar equations can be had with fathers-in-laws too but somehow mothers-in-laws are more infamous worldwide (don't take me wrong). Now, in these situations, nothing works between them. Neither of them tolerates the other and they are always seen on either side of a battleground.

How to deal with it?

When dealing with in-laws who are becoming a reason for conflict between couples, the major role is to be played by the partner whose parents are in question. They need to explain to them and let them know that there is no reason for their disapproval or disliking of their spouse. That he is happy with his partner and even they should look at their positives instead of pointing out their negatives always.

In case they still do not agree it should be made clear that their opinion does not matter and in no way would change their opinion or attitude towards their partner. Most intelligent parents would understand what they are talking about and also the hidden warning behind it and try to come to terms with them or else withdraw.

The same is the case with interfering in-laws. It should be communicated clearly to them and with kind words that they respect their concern but they would like to handle things themselves and their interference is only causing problems between them.

When you bind in marriage, you not only bind yourself with your partner but also his parents. So why not love and respect them? Would you not want your partner to respect your parents? Would you not feel bad if he badmouths them? If yes, then you should be respecting his parents too. Moreover, respect is one thing you owe to them for having brought up the person you love.

Treat them with kindness and try to understand their emotions when they want to spend time with their children. You will be able to take it more acceptingly when you put yourself in their shoes and try to look into your future when you would crave for your children's time and love.

Unless you are dealing with very troublesome in-laws, remember that their opinions are just opinions. You should not take what they think about you very negatively. Or if they are always giving their advice and tips, you should keep in mind that you always have the option to agree or not, to follow them or not, and also the option to not argue every time about them.

It may not be that easy, but when you nourish your mind with the thought that, "my relationship comes first", you will get the power to be a little more patient, a little more accepting. This little effort from your side can

keep your partner happy and your
relationship at peace.

. LACK OF PERSONAL SPACE OR TIME

Lack of personal space and time is also one of
the reasons for conflict between couples. This
is because personal space or 'me' time allows
you to relieve stress, rejuvenate yourself and
relax. It gives a sense of satisfaction or
fulfillment which is vital to keep your mind
balanced and at peace.

But if a partner neither enjoys a personal
space nor allows the other to have his own
personal time, then problems arise. It leads
to suffocation and frustration. Lack of
personal space causes you to feel irritated
which results in unnecessary arguments.

Lack of 'me' time causes your energy levels to
go down as you are never out of the
monotonous life you're leading. Change is
vital and lack of it may make you dull and
stressed. Such a life may make you feel
unhappy about your relationship and that
you were better before getting into it. Such

kind of negativity is sure to impact your daily lives, wherein bickering, blaming each other and criticizing becomes a ritual and ruins the relationship.

How to deal with it?

1. Give time to yourself

Harmony inside leads to harmony outside. If your head and heart are in harmony, you can maintain harmony in relationships. If a conflict between your head and heart is going on, there will be conflict outside.

Giving time to yourself makes you happy and gives you inner satisfaction and fulfillment. And this reflects in your behavior which ultimately affects your relationship in a positive fashion. Grooming yourself, engaging yourself in your favorite game or hobby, reading a book, or whatever gives you happiness. This little time you spend alone with yourself will help you discover your true self, and also help you understand and improve yourself as a person and thus improve your relationship.

I can understand that in busy schedules these days, it's difficult to find the time. But when you know the importance of this time and how it helps to heal your soul you will definitely try to make time for it. And you can begin by giving just ten minutes to yourself each day and gradually increase it, if possible. I'm sure that's not too much.

2. Give time to your friends and family

Being in a relationship does not mean you don't have a life beyond it. The friends, the family, and the people you knew or met before your marriage should still be a part of your life. Even things or activities you liked to do or places you liked to go are still important. Marriage does not mean breaking off from the outside world. This may cause serious damage to your soul or character.

You were an individual before your marriage and you should incorporate your marriage into your life in a healthy way, in a way that there is still 'the other' life left. You need to feed your soul.

3. Help your partner too

Soul healing is essential for your partner too. As important as it is to give yourself time, it's equally important to encourage your partner too to have a 'me' time or a social life or a life beyond the relationship.

There are times when your partner feels stuck or is going through a low phase in life like a career crisis. Often mothers of young children who have to stay back from work for a long time and are most of the time doing just childcare and household chores feel trapped and enter into this phase of post-partum depression. In such times you need to help your partner overcome their bad time by encouraging them to involve in activities that make them happy. During this time they need your support in healing their soul and going back to being who they are.

CONCLUSION

Now that you know the various reasons which made couples fight for ages and also how to go about them, you can try to overcome them. Also, it is extremely important to nourish your mind with the thought – 'Relationship comes first', so that conflicts do not take their place above your relationship in your life. All the reasons we have discussed above can be easily talked about and sorted only if you reset your mind with our approach.

. Relationship comes above our egos and conflicts

. Replace criticism with appreciation. Appreciate your partner every day.

. Try to do every day, one act to help or please your partner.

. Try to look at their positives and respect them.

#3 EXPECTATIONS

Michael and Linda were married for four years when they were blessed with a baby girl. Michael was the CEO of a finance company. He had an amiable personality and exceptional communication skills. His profession involved daily meetings and frequent parties and social gatherings. His business parties were all about high-status people, glamour, and show-off. Linda somehow didn't fit in or that's what Michael felt. Linda was a very simple girl. She worked as a content writer for a marketing agency. She was born and brought up in a mediocre family but with good values. Michael and Linda had met at the church at the wedding of a common family friend. Michael had immediately fallen for Linda. Her simplicity and her unattended beauty made her stand different from the rest. Michael was then going through his struggle days. A nine-to-five job and a part-time degree to upgrade his career graph. He was a down-to-earth person at that time and it was no doubt that he fell for Linda because as they started seeing each other he realized that Linda was an intelligent girl with a very strong character. He somehow related to her as he himself was a very ambitious person. He had plans for a very abundant life.

Linda also liked Michael and even their families approved of their relationship, thanks to the common friend who acted like the mediator between them. They got married. Michael earned just enough from his job to support their family and soon Linda also got her content writing job. They were very happy in the first three years of their marriage.

After one year of marriage, Michael completed his MBA and started giving job interviews. He got a few offers out of which he chose a finance company in which he saw potential growth. He got the position of Senior Manager there. With his expert management and communication skills, Michael climbed the ladder quite unexpectedly to reach the CEO's chair within three years. Linda was expecting their child then and the family celebrated his success.

But with success also came pride and self-importance. Michael started feeling that he was just too good at everything and maybe that Linda did not match up to him. This attitude came forward every time they had a business party or there were guests at home. Michael was always saying, "Why don't you groom yourself?" "Can't you dress up properly?" "You should try to learn from the other ladies at the party, the way they walk, the way they talk". And that's not all. They always came back from such events, quarreling. Michael had problems with everything. "You don't know what to say." "You looked so average, in no way like a CEO's wife". And Linda kept confronting her and said she has her own likes and her own way of doing things.

A few times Linda tried to dress up according to Michael's likings to make him happy, but that made her own self unhappy inside. She felt she was trying to be someone else or trying to be what she is not. She felt she was faking herself and killing her own personality and character.

On the other hand, she grew great disliking for Michael, who she felt had stopped loving her now and wanted her to be someone else or maybe even wants someone else to replace her in his life. She started doubting Michael about his loyalty and became insecure that he would very soon leave her for someone else, maybe someone more deserving. She lost all self-confidence and only found herself cursing her fate.

PROBLEM - Unrealistic expectations. Michael loves Linda but expects her to be a different person. Now, this is something like stealing away one's own character from oneself. He has no problem with her in their daily routine. Linda is a good wife and a mother and she is also doing well at her job. But when in society, he wants her to be someone else. As if he is ashamed to show the world that she is his wife.

According to Tony Robbins, "The problem with expectations in a relationship is that they're just an opinion: Everyone has one – and they don't always match up to the other person's thoughts."

We all have expectations. We expect the sun to rise every day and the seasons to change. This is because that's what we have seen and understood right from birth. So basically, expectations are our beliefs about how the world works. They may or may not be true, rational, or realistic.

So, what are realistic expectations in a relationship?

It's not true that you don't have the right to expect anything from your partner. Realistic expectations are simply those that can be met; others will only cause disappointment.

Expecting unconditional love and support from your partner, commitment in marriage, respect for each other, verbal affection, compassion, and empathy towards each other's feelings or interests are all examples of realistic expectations. Tony likes to call them standards rather than expectations.

But what if you expect your partner to do the laundry while you do the cooking? Is it not a realistic expectation? What's so unrealistic about it? It's totally normal to expect your partner to help you with the chores but you'll need to communicate what you expect. If both people assume the other person knows this automatically without ever having a conversation about it, it can lead to trouble.

Similarly, you can have expectations regarding finances, sex, splitting chores or giving time to each other or any other thing that is important to you but always remember to talk about your expectations. You should regularly have conversations about them as expectations keep changing.

Here it is also important that both the partners mutually agree upon it and it should not be a burden to one of the partners or something they find impossible to achieve. For instance, while dividing chores they should see each other's interests, so neither person is saddled with their most dreaded task.

Unrealistic expectations, on the other hand, are like wanting your partner to change their values, behavior, or interests or expecting them to be perfect, or expecting them to act or feel the same way you do or the way you want them to.

Now, these are unrealistic expectations. You are an individual and so is your partner. You cannot expect to share the same ideas, habits, behaviors, feelings, or character. Looking for a partner who is your own clone or replica or who fits into your definition is foolishness because you will never find one. Your existing partner is perhaps the best for you (at least when you start believing this, things will be much better). So, here we will talk about the most common expectations that couples tend to have with each other, which are unrealistic or mismatched.

Unrealistic expectations may be categorized under two heads, one that you have from your partner and the other you have from your relationship.

EXPECTATIONS FROM PARTNER

. Expecting partner to take care of things around the house

Although expectations regarding household tasks are not categorized under unreasonable expectations as these can be talked about and divided according to the availability or comfort of both partners, they may become unreasonable if one partner expects the other to do it all by themselves without trying to contribute to it in any way. Such expectation brings resentment and the partner gets the feeling of "I do it all" and this may give rise to frustrations and thus conflicts.

It's fine in case one partner is earning while the other is doing household chores or maybe childcare. But that doesn't mean the working partner has to depend on the other for even putting his shoes away or putting his plate in the sink. Such an attitude makes the other partner feel taken for granted.

What is to be done?

Little acts of service can not only be a great help to your partner in lightening their burden but also show them that you love them and care for them.

Learn to be empathetic towards others (not only your partner). This is a great virtue that will not only help you have a better relationship but also a better character.

. Expecting your partner to always subdue in case of a conflict

This is a very common expectation for those who have a high ego. Such people never want to call off an ongoing conflict or a cold war and always expect their partner to do so. I also believe that these people are highly patient or they strongly believe their partner will react according to their expectations or maybe they do not really care about their relationship.

Such an attitude firstly is totally wrong on their part because in a relationship, it is the responsibility of both partners to make efforts to keep it going and if they are not it clearly signals to the other partner their lack of dedication to their relationship.

Secondly, if one partner is always expected to say sorry or apologize or even call off a cold war, he or she may start getting the feeling of low or no self-respect. He will surely someday or the other be forced to choose his self-respect over his relationship and the relationship would suffer.

What is to be done?

It seems dreadful to be coming forward to end a conflict, but it's not that difficult. After all your partner would not fire a headshot in reply. All that's going to happen is that this effort from your side will most likely initiate a conversation that will help to clear out things or else just say, "forget it".

It is very easy and comfortable to sit back and see the other person come forward to smooth things over, but it needs a lot of courage. You have to fight your ego, sometimes even your self-respect to do this, to place your relationship above them, but it's totally worth it. Remember, your relationship comes above your egos and conflicts. So, the next time you get into a war, be brave enough to come forward to put your arms down.

. Expecting your partner to change or expecting they will never change

Frequently being asked to change one's behaviors or personality can impact one's self-esteem and sense of freedom. Just as it was in the case of Michael and Linda; where Michael wanted his wife to change her style or actions to match his polished business circle, and ultimately resulted in the loss of Linda's trust and security in her relationship

In the other case, it is not uncommon to see people expecting their partners to always look attractive. In expecting this they even forget the pain they inflict on their partner when they constantly nag them about their gained weight or their aging skin or those not-so-well-maintained locks. Our bodies and looks are bound to change with time. But refusing to accept this and wanting the partner to retain their looks throughout time is an unrealistic expectation.

What is to be done?

Accept and love your partner for what they are. You need to redefine the meaning of attraction. Try to look beyond physical aspects to see what really attracts you to your partner. Their beautiful inner side is what matters most and is much more important than physical beauty.

In the case of Michael and Linda, he needs to think about why he wants Linda to change, for himself or the society. The answer is clear. Society may have set beauty and lifestyle norms but it is up to us to accept them or follow them or not. I have seen several people who may not qualify the prevalent beauty norms but with their confidence, their personality, or sometimes just their beautiful smile they create such an enigma that draws people towards them and they take awe and inspiration from them.

. Expecting your partner to read your mind

You often hear couples complaining, "You knew I was upset, still you sat there scrolling your phone and did not care about me". The other partner is like, "when did you tell me that you were upset?"

It is very common to see couples expecting each other to read their minds. While it may happen to a certain extent as being a couple you tend to know how and when your partner reacts or feels in a certain way. But this may not always be true. So expecting your partner to always know what you are thinking or feeling and getting frustrated if they don't is an unrealistic expectation.

On the other hand, many partners not just rely on their partners to understand their feelings but also expect them to be always available when in distress. Your partner may or may not be available physically or mentally to comfort you on every occasion when you are upset. Sometimes they may not be in the right state of mind or may be preoccupied with other matters and may not be able to provide you that support.

Another case is when one partner always wants the other to be in agreement with him, or, in other words, he always wants to see them nodding their head at whatever they say or do.

William and Sarah went to their business parties and often came back yelling and shouting at each other. The last time when they went to one such party and William was giving his expert opinion on the most profitable stocks and Sarah happened to name another stock that was also doing well; William looked at her with a raised eyebrow and Sarah bit her tongue. William did not like Sarah interrupting him or placing her opinion when he was talking about something. He expected Sarah to always agree with what he was saying.

Now, this expectation is totally unrealistic as every individual has their own thoughts and perspectives and it is wrong to expect it will always match with yours. On the other hand, expecting your partner to keep quiet or not put their opinion forward is pathetic behavior.

What is to be done?

Instead of expecting the partner to know it all and end up disappointed, try to relate your feelings to them. This can lessen the chances of the two of you getting into a conflict.

Try to self-console instead of always relying on your partner. This actually is a good technique to become a strong character as well because you learn to fall and rise on your own without depending on anyone to support you.

Respecting your partner and respecting their feelings and opinions is vital for any relationship. In a partnership, both partners should have the right to place their opinion. They may or may not be in agreement with each other always. So, always ask each other if they agree while taking any decisions big or small to ensure that their voice is also heard.

. Expecting your partner to spend all their free time with you or expecting them to not have any friends especially the opposite sex

Relationship requires spending quality time with each other but what if a partner wants the other to give them all their free time? Then such a relationship becomes suffocating. This is a sign of unhealthy love and also shows insecurity. There is a need for personal space in every relationship as it gives a sense of satisfaction and the lack of it makes the relationship start feeling like a burden.

Expecting your partner to have no other friends than you may be like pulling or tugging your partner from their pre-relation life or individual life. Such a situation makes the partner feel that their relationship is taking the most of them and is pulling them away from your world beyond the relationship. This problem can especially be seen where partners are expected to not have friends of the opposite sex. This clearly signals a lack of trust and insecurity.

What is to be done?

It is important to strike a balance between spending time together and engaging in personal interests. It is like balancing your diet, Where spending time with each other is like the carbs (you need more of them) and your me-time is like the vitamins and minerals (you need them in very small quantities but cannot ignore them). Sticking to a schedule that involves all these necessary aspects can help to maintain this balance.

Instead of trying to pull your partner from their friends or people, try to work on your insecurities and on building trust in your relationship. You may drag a relationship for a while with your unrealistic expectations and by acting as your partner's watchdog but a long-term relationship can only be expected if you can blindly trust each other.

EXPECTATIONS FROM YOUR RELATIONSHIP

. Expecting your relationship to always be the same

Now, with such expectations, you are doing real harm to yourself and your relationship as you are sure to get disappointment.

Relationships change with time, as everythin else does. Change is inevitable. You may not always have the same "butterflies in the stomach" feeling that you had at the beginning of your relationship. The 'head ove heels' feeling is soon going to dissipate, and that's very obvious. The initial phase of that honeymoon period that is characterized by intense desire, love, and lust will soon give way to ease as you start getting comfortable with each other and soon become two ordinary people dealing with the reality of day-to-day life. So, expecting your relationship to always remain the same is unrealistic.

Similarly expecting that your partner will always be as romantic as they were at the beginning of the relationship is not practically possible. This is because we are different from what we really are, at the beginning of our relationship. Guys are a lot more romantic and girls look constantly attractive. But as life progresses and we get into life's daily struggles you can't really expect your guy to bring you flowers and compliment you as much as they used to or your girl to look hot after the daily chores. So, it's better to mind your expectations.

What is to be done?

Understand and accept the change time brings in your relationship. Appreciate the beauty of being with a person to whom you don't need to pretend or always present the best version of yourself. You can just be yourself and so can your partner.

Look at your relationship with a new dimension, what earlier was just attraction is now a beautiful bond where you both accept and appreciate each other's positives and negatives and also stand for each other and together move towards achieving the larger goals of your life.

At the same time work together to keep up the element of romance in your relationship because that shouldn't be missing altogether.

. Expecting to never have a conflict in your relationship

If you believe that happy marriage is all about never being in conflict with each other then I must tell you that you are living by a myth. Every marriage is bound to go through tough times and yours is not an exception. When two people live together they are bound to be in disagreement sometimes and it's normal.

That is because every individual comes from different backgrounds, cultures, and upbringing and has their own set of feelings and perspectives. They look at life from different angles so they are bound to differ on certain matters.

What is to be done?

Accept conflicts as a part of your relationship and do it gracefully. Conflicts bring with them the opportunity to evolve and grow in your relationship. It's the tough times of life that teach you the best lessons. It's during these times that partners learn to look at their shortcomings, learn to view things from their partner's perspective, and struggle together to find a way out. So, not only are conflicts inevitable but are also somehow important to enhance and strengthen our bond.

Fairy tales are good to read but one should not expect their life to be one. And if you want to, try your best to make it possible. If both partners put in the effort and prioritize their relationship above all, life can be somewhat of a fairy tale.

CONCLUSION

Expectations come in every relationship and they are normal. But you have to learn to control and never let those expectations overpower your relationship. Moreover idealizing your partner's image and expecting them to fit into that image is not the correct way of life. On the other hand, comparing your relationship with someone else's is also wrong. Every person and every relationship is different from the other.

So try to become more accepting and less expecting in your relationship. Be a little more kind, a little more forgiving, a little more loving, a little more giving, and see your bond grow stronger and better.

. Change is inevitable. Accept it as a part of your life.

. Talk about your expectations to your partner.

. Be brave enough to come forward to end a conflict, rather than always expecting your partner to do so.

#4   FAMILIES

James was brought up by his single mother. They had been through very tough times. James' father died when he was just four due to a massive heart attack. Since then Norah had been working day and night to make a living and ensure that James was brought up well. She had sacrificed a lot to make sure James went to the best college.

James was a disciplined boy and understood what her mom had been through. He excelled in his academics and procured a scholarship at the university.

James was an adult now and was almost over the miserable environment of his house. Of course, he felt bad for his mother but could not bear her stories of grief round the clock. He moved out to another city and soon started working for an IT company. Here he met Emma who was also a new recruit in his company. James and Emma became good friends as they were working in one team.

After about two years Emma moved to another city to pursue her master's while she kept in contact with

James. James continued in the same company and joined a part-time degree course. He soon got promoted and was now earning well. He also started sending money to her mother now.

Norah was happy about her son sending her money. But she felt lonely and wanted someone, someone to listen to her stories of misfortune and how she went through it all alone. She started entering into depression.

James and Emma now decided to tie a knot. They were happy. They moved into their new house and everything was smooth until James got a call from Norah's doctor, who said that Norah's condition was deteriorating and she cannot be left alone. James brought her home.

Emma could somehow not get along with Norah. She found her very irritating and kept complaining to James about her unhealthy and unclean habits. James knew her mom and just asked Emma to ignore her. But things kept growing and Emma as hard as she tried to tolerate Norah's disappointing behavior could not somehow get along with it.

It was when she got pregnant with James' baby that she decided finally that she could not share her house with his mother. To this James got furious at

Emma saying, "I understand your worries but why don't you just ignore her and believe she does not exist". Emma said, "It's easier said than done". She declared that either she would stay in the house or his mom.

James had no solution to this, so for the next few days, he tried to cut off from the situation and pretend as if nothing had happened. But, Emma caught him on one occasion and questioned him straight in his face, "So, what's your decision?" "What decision?" James said as if he didn't know what she was talking about. "You know what your mom did to me today? She spat the soup I gave her, saying that I was a horrible cook. I'll bring the soup to you and you tell me how it tastes." Emma went to the kitchen and returned with the bowl of soup. James took a little sip from the bowl, then went straight to his mom. He tried to explain to her that she would have to change her behavior and come to terms with Emma but as usual, Norah did not heed a word and only played the victim.

James then went over to Emma and said, "Honey, I know you are not wrong. I love you. But I can't leave my mom alone to die." Tears rolled down his eyes as he said this. And then as he continued to say, "You know what she has gone through, for me…."; Emma got up and left their house.

PROBLEM – Family

Sometimes it's not the conflict with the family, but the family itself that is the problem. Emma didn't have a conflict with James' mother. She knew quite well that Norah was in depression and she also felt sorry for her, but at the same time, she could not live with her. Maybe she felt that it was making her own life miserable. She knew that it was difficult for James; she knew his past, his struggle, and also his respect for his mom. But somehow she could not live this way.

James was in the worst situation. He wanted to be a loyal husband and also a loyal son but now he had to choose to be one of them. This dilemma was next to death for him. He loved his wife and could have done anything for her but he also had the responsibility of his aging mother. How could he shirk that responsibility? He owed her his whole life.

It's not that James didn't know whom he wanted to be with. When he was asked: 'Whose side are you on?' he knew he was on whose side, he wanted to scream and say "It's you" but he could not. And this dilemma which did not allow him to decide broke his marriage.

WHAT IS TO BE DONE?

When we bind together in a relationship, we almost make an unsaid promise to always prioritize our relationship above everything else and also our partner above everyone else. You may have conflicts among yourselves many a time but you always want your partner to take your side when someone else makes you uncomfortable, hurts you, or threatens you. Even if you feel somewhere inside that the person is not wrong; still, the last thing you expect from your partner is to take his side.

It's not always about who's right or who's wrong. Sometimes you just have to decide on whose side you stand. In marriage, there is this expectation that your partner will stand on your side leaving the whole world on the other side.

So is this expectation right or wrong? Is it realistic or unrealistic?

Let's say you are lucky enough to have never confronted a situation wherein you had to choose between two very important sides or roles of your life. Maybe you never had to choose between your wife and your mom for any reason; then you may call the above expectation unrealistic. That's because both are different parts of your life and both hold their own levels of importance to you. Because they never came in the way of each other you can play your role of a loyal husband and a loyal son alternatively and keep things at peace.

But what about James's situation; Can you say Emma was wrong to expect that her husband would stand by her side? For sure she did not want to bring up this dilemma in front of James. It was only when she felt that her life would be extremely problematic and miserable if they continued to live with his mom, that she decided that she has to find a way to have a peaceful and happy life. Can you say Emma was wrong to want to live a happy life?

Everyone wants to be happy. Everyone wants their home to be a place where one finds comfort and peace of mind. No one wants their children to be born in a miserable home and be brought up hearing their grandma's stories of grief. We struggle throughout our lives to make it happy and comfortable and we definitely deserve to be happy at the end of the day.

Of course, the pain and the sacrifice our parents may have gone through to give us what we have today or to make us what we are today cannot be forgotten. They are worthy of our love and respect and we ought to give them that. But if in some way even if it's unintentional they are depriving us of a happy married life, then we have to stop and think. Maybe it's time to make a decision.

Although leaving your parents or your family is always not the solution and is probably the last thing to do. Try to communicate individually with both sides of your relationship or you can even try sitting together to sort out the matter where both parties are allowed to put their opinions or feelings forward. Then you can try to create a common ground where both parties agree to meet. But I cannot guarantee you any great success from this practice because probably the matter is beyond communicational resolve else you may not have been given the option to decide upon one.

Although most people stuck up in similar situations choose to ignore the matter or detach from the situation or people or use 'stonewalling' as their armor, such techniques can only delay the matter and thi attempt which was meant to defuse the argument actually aggravates it.

Another way in which people often tend to react in such matters is by refusing to accept the partner's perspective. You may have ofter heard partners saying, "I don't really see a problem", "You are thinking way too much, take it easy" or "You know how she is, you have to accept it". Such denial of your perspective makes you question your place ir your partner's life. It gives you the clear message that either your partner is doubtful about the legitimacy of your feelings (maybe they feel you are lying or exaggerating things) or your feelings just don't mean anything to them. So, such efforts to bring peace to the situation will only create turmoil in your marriage as your partner will become doubtful about your core mutual feelings. This can be disastrous to your marriage.

Considering the fact that everyone deserves to be happy in life, it may be harsh to say but true that sometimes you have to place your relationship above your family too. It's your relationship you need to prioritize and you have to finally take this decision that you are on your partner's side. Anyways it has to be either side and yes it is wise to take this side to save your marriage.

I'll give you several reasons to justify this decision and make you feel a little less guilty.

Firstly you are committed to your partner to be with them through good times or bad. This is your testing time and frankly speaking, testing times are never easy that's why they are called so. So, if during such times you fail to prove your commitment to your partner, you break their trust and your relationship as well.

Secondly, your parents are in their later years of life and you and your partner have your whole lives in front of you. You cannot spoil it or deprive it of happiness just for the reason that you need to prove your loyalty as a son\daughter. To make your burden light I would even go on to say that had your parents been there at your place, they would have done the same.

If your children or their future are being affected by the ongoing conflict or situation, then surely you need to take this decision as you cannot spoil their future.

A relationship once broken may not be able to come back to life and this is not just going to affect the two people involved in it but also the children and also the two families associated with those two people. That means it will impact a lot of people. So, it's wise to choose your relationship above your family.

Failing in your relationship is probably one of the most painful experiences in life and your parents (if they truly are) cannot be indifferent to your pain. Your pain will definitely be theirs too. So, why inflict pain or so many people? Take it like this- A person develops a bad infection in one of the limbs and there is the risk of the infection spreading to the whole body. The doctors suggest amputating the limb. Now, this decision has to be made. The person knows the importance of his limb and what life would be without it. How he would manage his tasks without it? What his body would look like? That he would be incomplete without it. How would he be able to part with it? How painful it would be. A thousand

thoughts come to his mind, but he
takes this decision and he chooses t

Choosing to survive is the best option wh.
all other options are causing a threat to
survival. So for your relationship to survive,
remember – 'RELATIONSHIP SHOULD COME
FIRST'.

. In marriage, we are expected to take our
partner's side whenever a situation
demands so.

. It may be harsh to say, but true that
sometimes you even need to place your
relationship above your family.

For most of us, our phones are often the first and the last thing we see every day. Then how can we undermine its importance and the effect it has on every aspect of our life including our relationships? While social media has a few positive effects like helping us to stay in touch with our people (especially in case of long-distance relationships), helping us to share our relationships with the world and also get inspired by others, and helping us to make new friends, etc; It's strange how what's meant to connect us can actually disconnect us.

You may be thinking of it as a not-so-important topic to be discussed in this book but you will be shocked to know that social media is now becoming the latest and quite prominent reason for marriages failing. In a new study published in the scientific journal, "computers in human behavior", researchers have found that frequent social media use can do substantial harm to marital happiness and may sometimes even lead to divorce. Some of the findings of the study were as follows:

There was a 4% increase in the divorce rate, where Facebook usage had increased by 20%. Moreover, couples who used very less social media were found to be 11% happier in their marriage than those who used it frequently. Although these findings are not proof enough considering other factors involved, they still give a clear picture of the adverse effects of social media on our relationships. Today, it's being said that social media is the cause behind one in seven divorces.

The reason is that social media is not just a medium of entertainment, if it was, like our televisions or radios it would have not posed such a threat; but the fact that it opens or connects our lives to others, to the outside world. The sharing culture has reached the level where people don't dress up for themselves, but to get likes on social media. Family celebrations, weddings, and parties are now only a matter of photo shoots. Even a lunch or dinner date is about posting on Facebook or Instagram rather than spending some special moments with your loved one.

How social media affects relationships

1. Too much screen time

You must have often noticed how time just flies away when you pick up your phone to just check any updates, how an hour passes away when you ask your partner something while he is scrolling his phone and he says, "just one minute". This screen is actually addictive and has the power to hold you for hours without looking up. We have started spending more and more time with our phones and the result is that we are spending lesser time with our family and loved ones. Not only increased screen time leave us with less time to spend with our family but also reduce the quality of time we spend with them because they don't get our undivided attention and often partners are found competing with these screens for their partner's attention. This can become reason enough for conflict as they feel they are being ignored or not heard.

Often the person who is busy on the phone, maybe engrossed in an online game, when interrupted becomes irritated and the partne continuously trying to communicate may get aggressive and this may lead to conflict.

This social media addiction if left unchecked can cause a decline in our connection with the real world, particularly our partners. So, it's important to ensure we do not neglect our loved ones in favor of screen time.

2. Jealousy

Social media is the root cause of lower relationship satisfaction among couples these days. As couples see what other couples are doing or how happy they are (at least their posts show that); they tend to compare their relationship with others and blame or criticize each other for not being like them or doing things that others are.

For instance, if one couple goes out on a vacation and posts their "having a great time" pics on social media; it may result in other couples getting into conflict as they start feeling that they are not as happy as others are and start blaming, "you don't have time for me" or "why can't we go out?" or "when was the last time we went on a vacation?" and this creates the perfect environment for a conflict.

Jealousy can also arise when your partner is found to be in connection with their exes or someone you feel they may be attracted to. In such cases, spouses may get suspicious and start monitoring their partner's activities and interactions.

Trying to hide such connections in order to not hurt your partner can in turn become disastrous as hiding things from them will break trust and declare that you are at fault even if you are not.

On the other hand, social media is creating grounds for infidelity as people can maintain multiple connections and also have the option to look for better companions at hand. It's easier to get involved in relations online.

3. Disagreements related to social media

Often couples get into conflicts due to their disagreements or differences in social media behavior. For instance, they may fight over what to post and what not, or how to respond when they post something. Such conflicts are becoming common these days. Couples may differ in their levels of privacy and what they would like to share with the world. If these differences occur on a regular basis it may hurt the sentiments of the partner who wants to keep their private life private. On the other hand, the other partner may feel that they are being deprived of their independence and wishes.

Such disagreements can hurt feelings and lead to conflict.

WHAT IS TO BE DONE?

1. Fix your screen time

Too much screen time is not only bad for your relationship but for your health too. So, why not schedule a time for it? Not only will this be good for your health, but it will also save you a lot of time for yourself and your family. Moreover, only when we set an example by watching less phone can we expect our children to do it.

Fix a time for your family when you put your phones and computers away and just spend time with your loved ones. This is very important for better communication between the couple as their gadgets cause distraction and hinder quality communication.

Social media should also be a no-no at dinnertime and bedtime as firstly it is important from your health point of view and secondly this time should be reserved for the two of you or your family.

2. Think before you post

Keeping in mind what your partner feels is important when you post something on social media, especially if it's about the two of you or your relationship. Posting about some good romantic time you spent with your partner may hurt his sentiments or about some problems in your relationship can be extremely painful as such matters should be related to each other and sorted out personally rather than making it public.

Also posting some important news like maybe the news about being pregnant or getting a badly awaited promotion or sudden death of a relative or friend etc. can be disheartening if it hasn't been related to your partner. Your partner deserves to hear the news from you personally rather than learning it from your social media post.

3. Be open and honest

Never try to hide your social media connections or activities from your partner even if you think they won't like it. Trying to hide things will cause them to be even more suspicious and annoyed. On the other hand, communicating honestly with them about whom you have been connected with can make them understand and maybe even approve of it. If they struggle to approve of it, try to understand their feelings and stop what's making them upset. After all, it's your relationship and that's most important.

CONCLUSION

Social media does play an important role today as it has made connectivity very easy. But you need to watch before it disconnects you from your real world. These screens do not deserve the importance they are being given today. Life existed even before they were invented and can go on without them even now. Yes, it would definitely be difficult. But it is up to us to use them wisely to the limit that they make our life comfortable not to the limit that brings discomfort to our lives and our relationships. Relationships definitely come above social media.

. Schedule your family time that is gadget free.

. Do not hide your social media activities from your partner.

. Think before you post~ be responsible towards your relationship.

NOURISH YOUR MIND

Now that you have learned that relationships are the most important part of our lives, you may realize that making little sacrifices and compromises in a relationship is important at times and are not so difficult to be made.

A massive part of marriage and relationship success is putting your partner's needs before your own. Isn't it a very beautiful thought? Thinking about your partner before you think about yourself.

Let's face it relationships are not easy. It takes continuous efforts and commitment from both sides to become a happy or so-called "perfect couple".

You have to nurture your bond every day giving it adequate time, attention, and love and placing it above all other aspects of your life be it your profession, your ego, your conflicts, your family, or even sometimes your children. Yes, it may sound harsh but we cannot deprive ourselves of our intimate moments or times of togetherness just because of children. You have to together put in efforts to find a way out to steal time for yourself and you deserve it.

Learn to be more giving, and more forgiving in relationships. "It was his mistake", "Why should I talk to him?" these thoughts will only break, not make. And we are here to make. Isn't it?

At the same time apologizing for any wrong deed or behavior, not only saves your relationship but also satiates your guilt which is there even though your ego may not accept it. Remember that apologizing to your partner does not mean that you are wrong and the other person is right. It just means that you value your relationship more than your ego.

. Try to think about your partner before you think about yourself.

. Nurture your bond everyday with love, care and respect. Give your relationship the time it deserves.

. Think above your "ifs" and "whys" and place your relationship far above them.

START YOUR JOURNEY NOW

In this book, I told you about how your actions, your behavior, your habits, everything starts from your thoughts. I told you about the most powerful approach which is "Relationship comes first" with which you can refurbish your thought process and make your relationship a happy one and one that's destined to last a long -long time.

I hope you use the principles defined in this book to become your version of a perfect couple. I hope you remember and practice the exercises and affirmations suggested in this book to make your relationship better. If you wish to stay accountable in your journey, you can pick up "The Perfect Workbook – because relationships need some effort" by S. Aggarwal (available on amazon) which apart from reminding you the daily affirmations also helps you to make sure you are doing those little acts prescribed in this book, every single day to nourish your relationship. It is a nine-week workbook with daily practices, weekly goals to keep track of your progress and a final relationship report to make sure your efforts pay off. It is easy to use and would require just five minutes of your day. I'm sure that's not too much time. Remember you promised me to put in the effort. Your effort is vital to add meaning to whatever has been said in this book.

Marriage is not a project that will get over in a few weeks or a month or a year. It's a lifelong journey and it can never be perfect. Don't expect it to be perfect. Just go with the flow, enjoy the ups and downs and see how everything will ultimately pool into a beautiful journey of marriage.

'I'm not telling you it is going to be easy;

I'm just telling you it is going to be worth it.'

Happy Journey!

Buy "The Perfect Workbook –because relationships need some effort" on Amazon!

Feel free to contact me for your **free set of printable affirmations** that are beautifully designed so that they can be framed, to keep you motivated throughout your day. I'll be happy to send you the same.

e-mail me at: shrutifeb08@gmail.com

Made in the USA
Coppell, TX
15 September 2023